W9-BLM-821

Liam Hemsworth

By Alex Van Tol

Crabtree Publishing Company
www.crabtreebooks.com

Crabtree Publishing Company

www.crabtreebooks.com

Author: Alex Van Tol
Publishing plan research and development:
 Reagan Miller
Photo research: Tammy McGarr
Editor: Kathy Middleton
Proofreader and Indexer: Wendy Scavuzzo
Designer: Ken Wright
Production coordinator
 and prepress technician: Ken Wright
Print coordinator: Margaret Amy Salter

Photographs:
AP Images: Alex J. Berliner: p. 9; Diane Bondareff:
 pp. 18, 19
Everett Collection: © Lionsgate: p. 20
Getty Images: Kristian Dowling: p. 6; Michael Kovac:
 p. 8; Kevin Winter: p.10; Lester Cohen: p. 11;
 Marc Piasecki: p. 21
Keystone Press: © FAME Pictures: pp. 7, 26;
 © CARV/AKM-GSI: p. 25;
 © Nancy Kaszerman: p. 28
Photofest: © Walt Disney Pictures: p. 13;
 © Lionsgate: pp. 16, 17, 24
Shutterstock: © Featureflash: front cover; © s_bukley:
 title page, p. 15; © Jaguar PS: p. 5; © Creative Jen
 Designsp. 6 (inset); © DFree: pp. 22, 23
Superstock: MARVEL STUDIOS: p. 12
Thinkstock: Andreas Rentz: p. 4; Jason Merritt/Getty
 Images: p. 14; Charley Gallay/Getty Images: p. 27

Every effort has been made to trace copyright holders and to obtain their permission for use of copyright material. The authors and publishers would be pleased to rectify any error or omission in future editions. All the Internet addresses given in this book were correct at the time of going to press. The author and publishers regret any inconvenience caused if addresses have changed or sites have ceased to exist, but can accept no responsibility for any such changes.

Library and Archives Canada Cataloguing in Publication

Van Tol, Alex, author
 Liam Hemsworth / Alex Van Tol.

(Superstars!)
Includes index.
Issued in print and electronic formats.
ISBN 978-0-7787-8079-3 (bound).--ISBN 978-0-7787-8083-0 (pbk.).--
ISBN 978-1-4271-9985-0 (pdf).--ISBN 978-1-4271-9981-2 (html)

 1. Hemsworth, Liam, 1990- --Juvenile literature. 2. Motion picture actors and actresses--Australia--Biography--Juvenile literature. I. Title. II. Series: Superstars! (St. Catharines, Ont.)

PN3018.H46V36 2015   j791.4302'8092   C2014-907808-0
                                        C2014-907809-9

Library of Congress Cataloging-in-Publication Data

Van Tol, Alex, 1973-
 Liam Hemsworth / Alex Van Tol.
   pages cm. -- (Superstars!)
 Includes index.
 ISBN 978-0-7787-8079-3 (reinforced library binding) --
 ISBN 978-0-7787-8083-0 (pbk.) --
 ISBN 978-1-4271-9985-0 (electronic pdf) --
 ISBN 978-1-4271-9981-2 (electronic html)
 1. Hemsworth, Liam, 1990---Juvenile literature. 2. Actors--
Australia--Biography--Juvenile literature. I. Title.

 PN3018.H46V36 2015
 792.02'8092--dc23
 [B]
                                        2014045071

Crabtree Publishing Company

www.crabtreebooks.com   1-800-387-7650

Printed in Canada/042015/BF20150203

Published in Canada
Crabtree Publishing
616 Welland Ave.
St. Catharines, ON
L2M 5V6

Published in the United States
Crabtree Publishing
PMB 59051
350 Fifth Avenue, 59th Floor
New York, New York 10118

Published in the United Kingdom
Crabtree Publishing
Maritime House
Basin Road North, Hove
BN41 1WR

Published in Australia
Crabtree Publishing
3 Charles Street
Coburg North
VIC 3058

CONTENTS

Words that are defined in the glossary are in
bold type the first time they appear in the text.

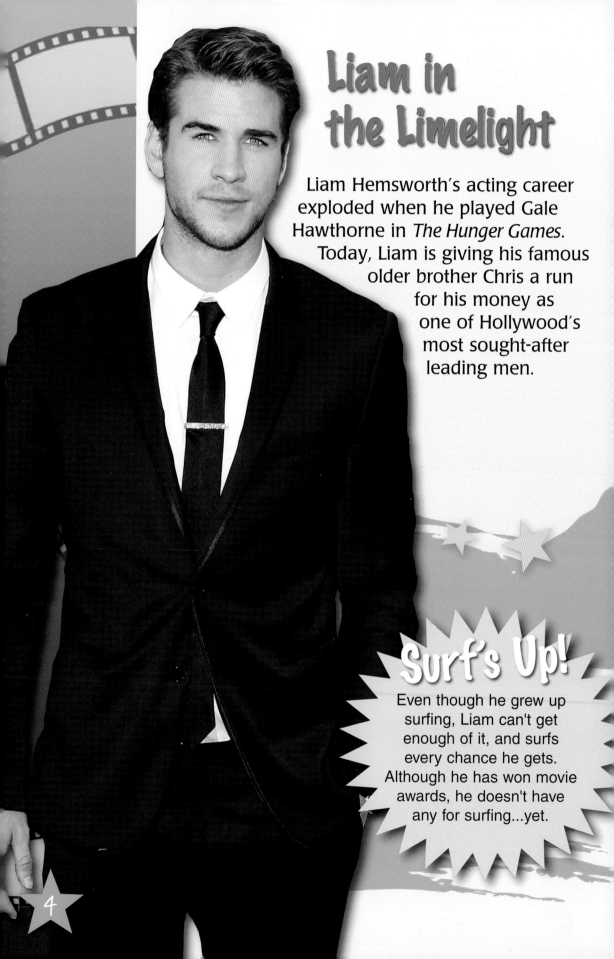

Liam in the Limelight

Liam Hemsworth's acting career exploded when he played Gale Hawthorne in *The Hunger Games*. Today, Liam is giving his famous older brother Chris a run for his money as one of Hollywood's most sought-after leading men.

Surf's Up!

Even though he grew up surfing, Liam can't get enough of it, and surfs every chance he gets. Although he has won movie awards, he doesn't have any for surfing...yet.

From Surfer to Silver Screen

Liam grew up in Australia, the youngest of three brothers. He wanted to be a pro surfer, but caught the acting bug from his older brothers. Roles on Australian TV dramas soon led to his big break in films. In 2010, Liam moved to Los Angeles and began **auditioning** for Hollywood movies. When he acted in *The Last Song* with Miley Cyrus, the two became a couple, and Liam was thrust into the spotlight. Their relationship boosted Liam's profile, and suddenly he was being considered for bigger roles.

Despite being fast-tracked to the bigtime with the success of *The Hunger Games* trilogy, Liam says he's still pretty grounded.

Life Down Under

Liam Hemsworth was born on January 13, 1990. He grew up in Melbourne, Australia. Liam is the baby of the family. His two older brothers Chris and Luke are actors, too. Liam is six years younger than Chris and nine years younger than Luke. His mother, Leonie, was an English teacher, and his father, Craig, worked as a counselor for children in child protective services. For most of their lives, the family lived in Melbourne, but they also spent some time in the rugged countryside of Australia called the outback.

Craig, Leonie, Chris, and Liam

Small-Town Childhood

When Liam was 13, the family moved to Phillip Island, located about two hours south of Melbourne. There were only about 7,000 people living on the island at that time. Their family life was pretty isolated, with no other kids close by. The boys played with each other and mostly entertained themselves by surfing. They were a rough-and-tumble bunch, playing with wooden swords, guns, and ninja stars given to them by their grandfather. Chris and Luke used to make Liam put on a couple of heavy sweaters, then stalk him around the backyard and attack!

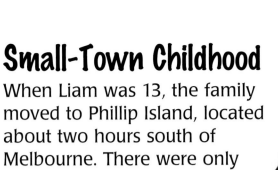

Liam got his mother's help to go furniture shopping in 2013 in Santa Monica.

Embarrassing Moments

Liam's mother was his English teacher for two years in high school. She was also the sex education teacher—awkward! Liam has said he used to keep his head down on the desk during those classes.

Rough and Tough

The rivalry between Liam and Chris was epic. They used to wrap towels around their hands and use them as gloves for boxing in the family room. They even got into physical fights to see who got to sit in the front seat of the car. When Liam's parents went away to Europe for three months, Luke and Liam stayed with their grandmother while Chris stayed with an uncle. Liam says he and Chris were too much trouble for their grandmother to take care of at the same time. One time, his poor mother even broke her finger trying to split the boys up during a fight!

At the end of the day, Liam and Chris are still brothers— and the family ties will always keep them tight.

He Said It

"I was the naughtiest brat as a child; my grandpa gave my brother the kind of knife you can throw at a tree and it will stick, but I threw it at Chris's head one day and luckily only the handle hit him in the forehead!"
—Interview in *Sydney Morning Herald*, March 18, 2012

Sibling Rivalry

Liam's oldest brother Luke got into acting first, then Chris. Liam used to watch them on TV shows. One day in high school, he decided to go along to the set of one show to watch Chris work. Liam says it sparked something inside him. At the age of 16, he decided to take acting classes, too, and started auditioning for shows. Today, the three brothers all live in Hollywood and actually compete with one another for film roles. But that's nothing new.

Shown here with Chris (center) and Luke (right), Liam says his older brothers always felt like he "got away with everything" because he was the baby of the family.

First Acting Roles

After graduating high school, Liam worked with Luke installing floors for six months, earning $15 an hour. It was during that time that the teenager landed his first guest spots on two of Australia's most popular TV series, *Home and Away* and *McLeod's Daughters*.

A Player

In *The Elephant Princess*, Liam played Marcus, the guitar player in the band. Turns out Liam can actually play!

Soaps and Series

It wasn't too long before Liam got his first big break in acting. His brother Luke had played a regular character on the Australian TV soap opera *Neighbours*. His brother Chris had also appeared in an episode of the show. In 2007, Liam followed in the family tradition and landed a **recurring** role on the series. He played the role of athlete Josh Taylor, who had become a paraplegic after losing the use of his legs in a surfing accident. Liam played Josh for 27 episodes. His television career began to take off in Australia, and he won roles in other TV shows, including the children's series *The Elephant Princess* and a series for adults called *Satisfaction*.

Hitting the Big Time

In 2009, the film world was also starting to discover this talented young Aussie. In Liam's first film role, he played a character that was murdered over and over again in the British horror film *Triangle*. He even won a role in Sylvester Stallone's film *The Expendables*. Things were looking good, so he decided to move to California to join his brother Chris in pursuing acting on the big screen.

Liam was so excited to meet Sylvester Stallone. He had watched all of his movies growing up, especially the *Rocky* and *Rambo* series.

He Said It

"I remember standing in my living room and seeing a Rocky *DVD on my shelf and talking to [Sylvester Stallone] at the same time and thinking, 'This is bizarre.'"*
—Interview in Sydney Morning Herald, March 18, 2012

Who Gets to Play a God?

Liam and Chris shared the same manager in those early days. Unfortunately, it meant the competitive brothers were sometimes sent to audition for the same parts. When the title role in the movie *Thor* came up, Liam auditioned for the role after Chris had read for the part. Chris was not called back, but Liam made the list of the top five finalists. But in a true Hollywood ending, Liam lost the role…to Chris! Not even in the final five, Liam's lucky older brother landed two movie roles that same week. (The other role was in the film *Red Dawn*.) On top of that, Liam had found out that his character was being cut from *The Expendables* before filming even started. Liam remembers sitting in their manager's guest house, where the brothers were living at the time. Downhearted, he thought he might have to return home to Australia if he didn't land a part soon. But Liam's luck was about to change.

Turns out it was big brother Chris, and not Liam, who got to swing Thor's hammer.

The Turning Point

Just a few weeks later, Liam found out he had won a leading role opposite Miley Cyrus in the movie *The Last Song*. He got the job when he had only been in Los Angeles for three weeks! In *The Last Song*, Liam plays the role of mechanic and volleyball player Will Blakelee. His character falls for the edgy, rebellious piano prodigy Ronnie Miller, played by Miley Cyrus. When the movie came out in 2010, Liam won numerous awards for his performance.

Serious Cyrus

Meeting Miley Cyrus was a strange feeling for Liam. After he auditioned for *The Last Song* in 2009, he called up his brother Chris to share how weird it was to meet the Disney star after having grown up watching her on television in *Hannah Montana*.

Liam and Miley worked together on location in Savannah and on Tybee Island, both in Georgia.

Love Bites

During the filming of *The Last Song*, Liam and Miley got to know each other well. They were filming together every day. Neither one of them had friends in Georgia, where they were filming, and they hung out together much of the time. It's no wonder they fell in love! When they began dating, Liam was 19, and Miley was 16.

Only Human

Two and a half years after first falling head over heels, Liam and Miley became engaged, in May 2012. "When you're filming those scenes with someone and pretending to love them, you're not human if you don't feel something," Liam has said.

By the time the couple became engaged, Miley was 19 and Liam was 22.

Coming Home to Hollywood

When Liam returned to Los Angeles with Miley Cyrus, the **paparazzi** were excited to have a new celebrity couple to watch. Being on the covers of so many celebrity magazines, Liam's star began to rise super fast. He started getting more attention from casting directors, too.

Liam and Miley lived together in Los Angeles for a short while following their engagement.

The Lady for Liam

Liam and Miley became engaged in 2012. They sealed their commitment with new tattoos, sharing a quote from a speech by US President Theodore Roosevelt. Liam's reads, "if he fails, at least fails while daring greatly." Miley's tattoo finishes the quote, "so that his place shall never be with those cold and timid souls who knew neither history nor defeat." Unfortunately, the couple broke up in 2013. Though it was difficult at the time, the two have remained on good terms.

The Role of a Lifetime

With a leading film role now under his belt, Liam got a call in March 2011. He was half asleep when he answered the phone, but he was wide awake a few seconds later: director Gary Ross said Liam had done a great job of reading for the upcoming movie **adaptation** of *The Hunger Games*, the popular young-adult book series by author Suzanne Collins. He offered Liam a major role in the movie! It was an invitation that would change his life.

By the Book

Before he even auditioned for the role of Gale Hawthorne, Liam read all three books in the trilogy. He wanted to do the role justice by staying very true to the book.

Getting Behind Gale

The Hunger Games is a story set in the future in a **post-apocalyptic** North America. Young adults are made to compete against each other to the death in the wilderness as television entertainment. In the movie, Liam was cast as Gale Hawthorne opposite rising star Jennifer Lawrence, who would play Katniss Everdeen. Gale is Katniss's childhood friend, and he agrees to look after her family while she fights for her community. Liam felt close to the role because Gale Hawthorne was passionate about standing up for what he believes in, something that has always been a big part of Liam's own life.

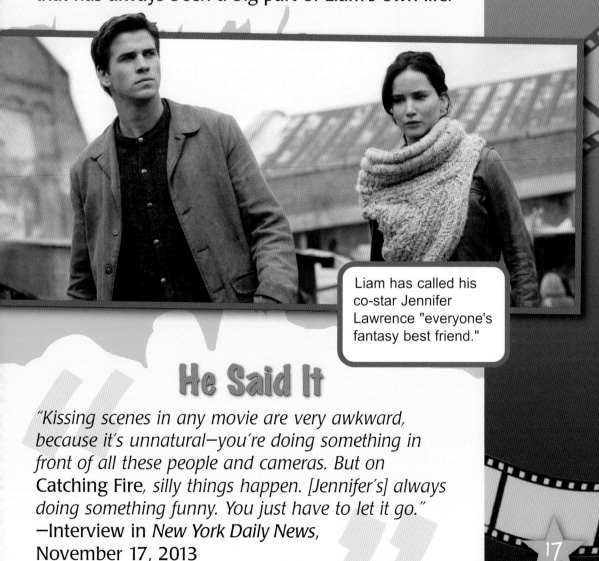

Liam has called his co-star Jennifer Lawrence "everyone's fantasy best friend."

He Said It

"Kissing scenes in any movie are very awkward, because it's unnatural—you're doing something in front of all these people and cameras. But on Catching Fire*, silly things happen. [Jennifer's] always doing something funny. You just have to let it go."*
—Interview in *New York Daily News*, November 17, 2013

Epic Training

Liam began preparing for the role at once. Since food is scarce in the futuristic world of *The Hunger Games*, he wanted to get into both the physical and mental state of a character who has spent most of his life hungry. Liam trained with a former Navy SEAL for 90 minutes a day, five or six days a week, throwing around tires, ropes—anything to keep his heart pounding and his fat burning. Luckily, Liam really enjoys working out. It helps prevent him from gaining weight after bingeing on his favorite treat: Krispy Kreme donuts.

It's not enough for Liam to pedal a spin bike or run on the treadmill. For him, the best part of cardio is having fun!

Grumpy as Gale

The strict training helped him drop about 20 pounds before filming began. To get the overly lean body of a starving man, he followed a very limited diet. Liam says he felt hungry nearly all the time, and it made him really grumpy. It helped him understand how the character Gale Hawthorne might feel and act. But he missed his favorite foods. If he had his way, he'd eat pizza and burgers for the rest of his life!

On Kicking Butt with Katniss

Liam really enjoyed working with Jennifer Lawrence filming *The Hunger Games* series. He finds her to be very caring toward the people around her and says she's one of the best actresses he has ever worked with. He enjoys how she approaches her work— "without a filter" is how Liam puts it. When she's on set, Jennifer just says whatever is on her mind, and she often surprises her costars by the funny things she says just before a scene starts shooting. Liam thinks Jennifer was born to play the heroine of *The Hunger Games* trilogy.

He Said It

"I love going to the gym, sweating, running around, feeling like I'm having a heart attack. I like the physical side of boxing—it's fun to punch a bag for 20 minutes—but I also feel mentally strong when I box. I feel good in my own body."
—Interview in *Men's Health*, September 2012

19

Toughening Up

Liam was now an actor with some star power, and Sylvester Stallone couldn't help but notice. Cut from the first *The Expendables* movie, Stallone put Liam's character back in for the sequel, *The Expendables 2*. Liam was ecstatic. He got to work with tough-guy actors Sylvester Stallone, Bruce Willis, Arnold Schwarzenegger, and Jean-Claude Van Damme. Playing the team's newest recruit, Billy "The Kid" Timmons, Liam's character helps the group of **mercenaries** defeat a bad guy threatening the world. For the role, Liam had to gain back all the weight he had lost playing Gale Hawthorne. Happily for him, oatmeal, brown rice, fish, chicken stirfry, and scrambled eggs were suddenly the order of the day.

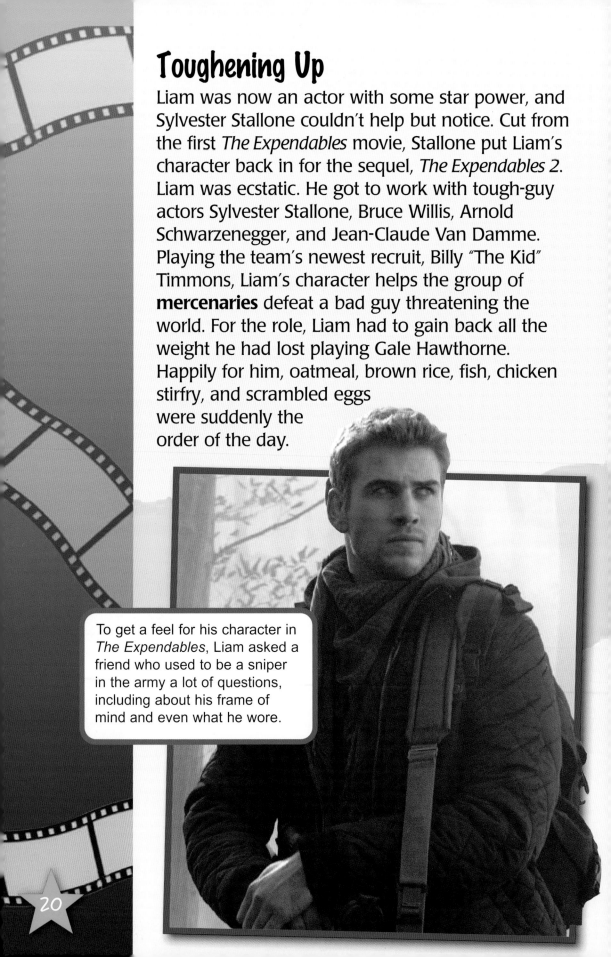

To get a feel for his character in *The Expendables*, Liam asked a friend who used to be a sniper in the army a lot of questions, including about his frame of mind and even what he wore.

Hard Work Pays Off

Liam is extremely diligent and serious about his work. He has the same work ethic as his favorite actors Heath Ledger, Leonardo DiCaprio, and Paul Newman—actors known to be very serious about their craft. Liam believes if you're willing to put in the hard work, then you will be successful in the end. But it's a tough job when you're constantly under public **scrutiny**—and this is the part Liam has trouble with. When he was filming *Paranoia*, Liam asked costar Harrison Ford whether he ever doubted what he was doing or why he was doing it. Ford told him he didn't. Acting, he said, is the best job in the world.

Danger Man

Liam is no stranger to danger. In 2014, he jumped out of an airplane! The free fall didn't stress him out because things happened so fast, there wasn't any time to think about it. He said he felt the most fear when he was floating back to Earth.

Liam happily greets fans at the premiere in Paris of *The Hunger Games: Catching Fire*.

21

Working With Friends

As Liam got to know the cast of *The Hunger Games*, he established comfortable friendships with them. He has become fast friends with Josh Hutcherson who plays the role of Peeta, with whom Katniss fights side by side in the first film. There were a lot of laughs on set when Liam, Josh, and Jennifer were around! Liam says it was a bit like high school, with people trying to trip each other up during a scene. Liam also has tremendous admiration for actor Woody Harrelson, who plays Katniss's **mentor**, Haymitch Abernathy.

Love for Liam

Liam's female costars have nothing but praise for him. Melissa George (*Triangle*) says he is easy to get along with, and he was always willing to stay late to perfect a scene. Jennifer Lawrence (*The Hunger Games*) says he is laid-back, honest, and funny. And Teresa Palmer (*Love and Honor*) says his generosity, energy, and talent make him a natural leader.

Elizabeth Banks, Liam Hemsworth, Jennifer Lawrence and Josh Hutcherson arrive at *The Hunger Games: Catching Fire* premiere in Los Angeles.

Busy Times

Recent years have been busy for Liam. In 2012, he shot *Empire State*, where he played a young security guard whose best friend convinces him they should rob the armored car depository. Liam also acted in *Paranoia*, a thriller about a young man whose boss blackmails him into spying on the competition. Last, but certainly not least, 2012 also saw him shooting *The Hunger Games: Catching Fire*. And the fast pace continues even now. Liam has gone straight from shooting one movie to the next without a break. He says it has been a tremendous workload, but he feels very lucky—and thankful.

Liam has shown he is capable of playing many varied roles.

Giving Back

Liam is an ambassador for the Australian Childhood Foundation, along with his brother, Chris. The organization helps children who are living in situations of **trauma**, neglect, and abuse. Liam feels fortunate having enjoyed a safe and loving childhood. It grounded him and provided the foundation for his current success. Liam uses his Twitter feed and his Facebook page to post updates about the good work the organization is doing, and to encourage others to lend a hand, too. He has tweeted videos from the Australian Childhood Foundation, and shared a UNICEF plea for pledges to support disaster relief after **Typhoon** Haiyan damaged the Philippines.

He Said It

"I have the best parents you can have. They have worked in child protection for twenty years and have only ever given me encouragement and support, and I always felt safe and loved. The world is a scary enough place as it is for children. It is important that home should always be a safe place for them. If they don't have that, if they grow up unsafe and uncared for, that causes so much harm. I want the best for the next generation, because they are the future."
—On www.childhood.org.au, Australian Childhood Foundation

Celebrity Fundraising

When another friend nominated him, Liam accepted the Ice Bucket Challenge to help raise awareness for ALS (a disease that gradually paralyzes its victims). He showed up for his Ice Bucket Challenge dressed in a *Teenage Mutant Ninja Turtles* bodysuit! He was in the middle of explaining the challenge when he was unexpectedly soaked by the bucket of icy water, but he handled it with good humor. He nominated his *Hunger Games* costar Josh Hutcherson to take the challenge next. Celebrities such as Liam have helped to raise millions of dollars toward finding a cure for ALS.

Hunger Games star Jennifer Lawrence has praised Liam and his costar Josh Hutcherson, saying the two guys are her angels. (She called them kittens, too!)

Who's Your Uncle?

Liam has four nieces and two nephews. His brother Luke has three daughters, and his brother Chris has one daughter and twin sons. He loves his nieces and nephews, but isn't exactly lining up to be considered as the family babysitter. He hasn't ever changed a diaper yet, and is happy to keep it that way for now! Liam enjoys watching his brothers raise their families and has said he would like to be a good role model for children.

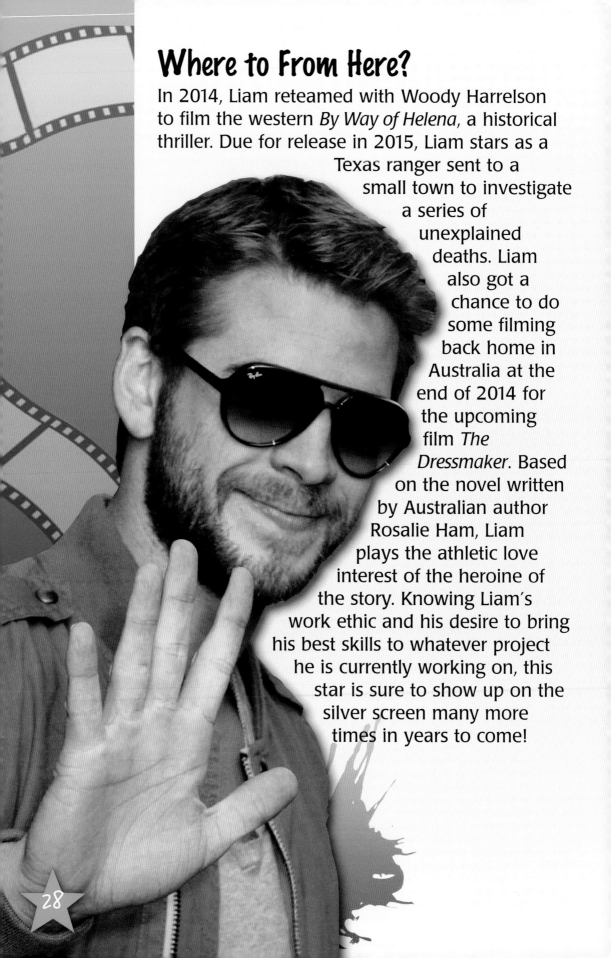

Where to From Here?

In 2014, Liam reteamed with Woody Harrelson to film the western *By Way of Helena*, a historical thriller. Due for release in 2015, Liam stars as a Texas ranger sent to a small town to investigate a series of unexplained deaths. Liam also got a chance to do some filming back home in Australia at the end of 2014 for the upcoming film *The Dressmaker*. Based on the novel written by Australian author Rosalie Ham, Liam plays the athletic love interest of the heroine of the story. Knowing Liam's work ethic and his desire to bring his best skills to whatever project he is currently working on, this star is sure to show up on the silver screen many more times in years to come!

Timeline

1990: Liam Hemsworth is born on January 13 in Melbourne, Australia.

2006: Sixteen-year-old Liam scores his first audition for *Home and Away*

2007: He graduates high school.

2007: Liam begins filming for the Australian soap opera *Neighbours*.

2008: Liam plays Marcus on the children's TV show *The Elephant Princess*.

2009: Sylvester Stallone gives Liam a role in *The Expendables*. Liam moves to Los Angeles.

2009: Liam auditions for the role of Thor, and lands a role in *The Last Song* with Miley Cyrus.

2009: Miley Cyrus and Liam film Miley's music video for the song "When I Look At You."

2010: Liam is written out of *The Expendables* and loses the title role in *Thor* to his brother Chris (2011).

2010: *The Last Song* wins Liam several awards

2011: Liam is cast as Gale Hawthorne in *The Hunger Games*.

2012: Liam kicks butt in *The Expendables 2*.

2013: *The Hunger Games*: *Catching Fire* is released.

2014: Liam is busy filming both parts of *The Hunger Games: Mockingjay*.

2015: Release date of film *By Way of Helena*.

2015: October release date of upcoming film *The Dressmaker*.

Glossary

adaptation A book or other written work that has been rewritten as a film

audition A short performance where an actor can show his/her talents when being considered for a part in a play or movie

mentor An adviser or teacher, similar to a role model

mercenary A soldier who fights for whoever hires him or her

paparazzi Photographers who take pictures of celebrities, usually when they're involved in living their day-to-day life

post-apocalyptic Relating to a time following a catastrophic event that ruins the world

recurring Happening again and again

scrutiny Critical observation or examination

trauma Damage to the psyche (mind and spirit) resulting from a severely distressing event

typhoon A large and powerful storm that develops in the ocean particularly near the Philippines and the China Sea

Find Out More

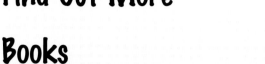

Books

Edwards, Posy. *Liam Hemsworth: Star of The Hunger Games*. Orion, 2012.

Shaffer, Jody Jensen. *Liam Hemsworth: The Hunger Games' Strong Survivor*. Lerner Publishing Group, 2013.

Tieck, Sarah. *Liam Hemsworth: Star of The Hunger Games*. Big Buddy Books, 2013.

Websites

IMDb
www.imdb.com/name/nm2955013/ bio?ref_=nm_ov_bio_sm
Liam's biography at IMDb

Australian Childhood Foundation
www.childhood.org.au

Liam on Twitter
https://twitter.com/LiamHemsworth

Biography of Liam Hemsworth
www.people.com/people/ liam_hemsworth/biography/

Liam Hemsworth bio at Kidzworld.com
www.kidzworld.com/article/25902- liam-hemsworth-bio

Index

About the Author

Liam Hemsworth is author Alex Van Tol's thirteenth book for young readers and her third biography. Once a middle school teacher, Alex now makes her living as a writer and editor. Alex is currently at work on a historical novel for adults. She lives right next to the beach in Victoria, BC.